A STATEM1
CATHOLIC BISHOPS OF THE
UNITED STATES

GLOBAL CLIMATE CHANGE

a plea for dialogue prudence and the common good

United States Conference of
Catholic Bishops

Washington, DC

The text for *Global Climate Change: A Plea for Dialogue, Prudence, and the Common Good* originated from the Domestic and International Policy Committees and was prepared in consultation with the bishops' Committee on Doctrine and the Committee on Science and Human Values. The document was approved for publication by the full body of US Catholic bishops at their June 2001 General Meeting and has been authorized by the undersigned.

Msgr. William P. Fay
General Secretary
USCCB

Photos: cover image © CORBIS/Eye on Earth Collection

Also available in Spanish: pub. no. 5-855.

First Printing, July 2001
Fourth Printing, October 2017

ISBN 978-1-57455-431-1

Contents

Introduction

A S PEOPLE OF FAITH, we are convinced that "the earth is the Lord's and all it holds" (Ps 24:1). Our Creator has given us the gift of creation: the air we breathe, the water that sustains life, the fruits of the land that nourish us, and the entire web of life without which human life cannot flourish. All of this God created and found "very good." We believe our response to global climate change should be a sign of our respect for God's creation.

The continuing debate about how the United States is responding to questions and challenges surrounding global climate change is a test and an opportunity for our nation and the entire Catholic community. As bishops, we are not scientists or public policymakers. We enter this debate not to embrace a particular treaty, nor to urge particular technical solutions, but to call for a different kind of national discussion. Much of the debate on global climate change seems polarized and partisan. Science is too often used as a weapon, not as a source of wisdom. Various interests use the airwaves and political process to minimize or exaggerate the challenges we face. The search for the common good and the voices of poor people and poor countries sometimes are neglected.

At its core, global climate change is not about economic theory or political platforms, nor about partisan advantage or interest group pressures. It is about the future of God's creation and the one human family. It is about protecting both "the human environment" and the natural environment.[1] It is about our human stewardship of God's creation and our responsibility to those who come after us. With these reflections, we seek to offer a word of caution and a plea for genuine dialogue as the United States and other nations face decisions about how best to respond to the challenges of global climate change.

The dialogue and our response to the challenge of climate change must be rooted in the virtue of prudence. While some uncertainty remains, most experts agree that something significant is happening to the atmosphere. Human behavior and activity are, according to the most recent findings of the international scientific bodies charged with assessing climate change, contributing to a warming of the earth's climate. Although debate continues about the extent and impact of this warming, it could be quite serious (see p. 19, The Science of Global Climate Change). Consequently, it seems prudent not only to continue to research and monitor this phenomenon, but to take steps now to mitigate possible negative effects in the future.

As Catholic bishops, we seek to offer a distinctively religious and moral perspective to what is necessarily a complicated scientific, economic, and political discussion. Ethical questions lie at the heart of the challenges facing us. Pope John Paul II insists, "We face a fundamental question which can be described as both ethical and ecological. How can accelerated development be prevented from turning against man? How can one prevent disasters that destroy the environment and threaten all forms of life, and how can the negative consequences that have already occurred be remedied?"[2]

Because of the blessings God has bestowed on our nation and the power it possesses, the United States bears a special responsibility in its stewardship of God's creation to shape responses that serve the entire human family. As pastors, teachers, and citizens, we bishops seek to contribute to our national dialogue by examining the ethical implications of climate change. We offer some themes from Catholic social teaching that could help to shape this dialogue, and we suggest some directions for the debate and public policy decisions that face us. We do so with great respect for the work of the scientists, diplomats, business and union representatives, developers of new technologies, environmental leaders, and policymakers who have been struggling with the difficult questions of climate change for many years.

While our own growing awareness of this problem has come in part from scientific research and the public debate about the human contribution to climate change, we are also responding to the appeals of the Church in other parts of the world. Along with Pope John Paul II, church leaders in developing countries—who fear that affluent nations will mute their voices and ignore their needs—have expressed their concerns about how this global challenge will affect their people and their environment. We also hear the call of Catholic youth and other young people to protect the environment.

Therefore, we especially want to focus on the needs of the poor, the weak, and the vulnerable in a debate often dominated by more powerful interests. Inaction and inadequate or misguided responses to climate change will likely place even greater burdens on already desperately poor peoples. Action to mitigate global climate change must be built upon a foundation of social and economic justice that does not put the poor at greater risk or place disproportionate and unfair burdens on developing nations.

Scientific Knowledge and the Virtue of Prudence

A S CATHOLIC BISHOPS, we make no independent judgment on the plausibility of "global warming." Rather, we accept the consensus findings of so many scientists and the conclusions of the Intergovernmental Panel on Climate Change (IPCC) as a basis for continued research and prudent action (see p. 19, The Science of Global Climate Change). Scientists engaged in this research consistently acknowledge the difficulties of accurate measurement and forecasting. Models of measurement evolve and vary in reliability. Researchers and advocates on all sides of the issue often have stakes in policy outcomes, as do advocates of various courses of public policy. News reports can oversimplify findings or focus on controversy rather than areas of consensus. Accordingly, interpretation of scientific data and conclusions in public discussion can be difficult and contentious matters.

Responsible scientific research is always careful to recognize uncertainty and is modest in its claims. Yet over the past few decades, the evidence of global climate change and the emerging scientific consensus about the human impact on this process have led many governments to reach the conclusion that they need to invest time, money, and political will to address the problem through collective international action.

The virtue of prudence is paramount in addressing climate change. This virtue is not only a necessary one for individuals in leading morally good lives, but is also vital to the moral health of the larger community. Prudence is intelligence applied to our actions. It allows us to discern what constitutes the common good in a given situation. Prudence requires a deliberate and reflective process that aids in the shaping of the commu-nity's conscience. Prudence not only helps us identify the principles at stake in a given issue, but also moves us to adopt courses of action to protect the common good. Prudence is not, as popularly thought, simply a cautious and safe approach to decisions. Rather, it is a thoughtful, deliberate, and reasoned basis for taking or avoiding action to achieve a moral good.

In facing climate change, what we already know requires a response; it cannot be easily dismissed. Significant levels of scientific consensus—even in a situation with less than full certainty, where the consequences of not acting are serious—justifies, indeed can obligate, our taking action intended to avert potential dangers. In other words, if enough evidence indicates that the present course of action could jeopardize humankind's well-being, prudence dictates taking mitigating or preventative action.

This responsibility weighs more heavily upon those with the power to act because the threats are often greatest for those who lack similar power, namely, vulnerable poor populations, as well as future generations. According to reports of the IPCC, significant delays in addressing climate change may compound the problem and make future remedies more difficult, painful, and costly. On the other hand, the impact of prudent actions today can potentially improve the situation over time, avoiding more sweeping action in the future.

Climate Change and Catholic Social Teaching

G OD HAS ENDOWED HUMANITY with reason and ingenuity that distinguish us from other creatures. Ingenuity and creativity have enabled us to make remarkable advances and can help us address the problem of global climate change; however, we have not always used these endowments wisely. Past actions have produced both good works and harmful ones, as well as unforseen or unintended consequences. Now we face two central moral questions:

(1) How are we to fulfill God's call to be stewards of creation in an age when we may have the capacity to alter that creation significantly, and perhaps irrevocably?

(2) How can we as a "family of nations" exercise stewardship in a way that respects and protects the integrity of God's creation and provides for the common good, as well as for economic and social progress based on justice?

Catholic social teaching provides several themes and values that can help answer these questions.

THE UNIVERSAL COMMON GOOD

Global climate is by its very nature a part of the planetary commons. The earth's atmosphere encompasses all people, creatures, and habitats. The melting of ice sheets and glaciers, the destruction of rain forests, and the pollution of water in one place can have environmental impacts elsewhere. As Pope John Paul II has said, "*We cannot interfere in one area of the ecosystem without paying due attention both to the consequences of such interference in other areas and to the well being of future generations.*"[3] Responses to global climate change should reflect our interdependence and common responsibility for the future of our planet. Individual nations must measure their own self-interest against the greater common good and contribute equitably to global solutions.

STEWARDSHIP OF GOD'S CREATION AND THE RIGHT TO ECONOMIC INITIATIVE AND PRIVATE PROPERTY

Freedom and the capacity for moral decision making are central to what it means to be human. Stewardship—defined in this case as the ability to exercise moral responsibility to care for the environment—requires freedom to act. Significant aspects of this stewardship include the right to private initiative, the ownership of property, and the exercise of responsible freedom in the economic sector. Stewardship requires a careful protection of the environment and calls us to use our intelligence "to discover the earth's productive potential and the many different ways in which human needs can be satisfied."[4]

We believe economic freedom, initiative, and creativity are essential to help our nation find effective ways to address climate change. The United States' history of economic, technological innovation, and entrepreneurship invites us to move beyond status quo responses to this challenge. In addition, the right to private property is matched by the responsibility to use what we own to serve the common good. Our Catholic tradition speaks of a "social mortgage" on property and, in this context, calls us to be good stewards of the earth.[5] It also calls us to use the gifts we have been given to protect human life and dignity, and to exercise our care for God's creation.

True stewardship requires changes in human actions—both in moral behavior and technical advancement. Our religious tradition has always urged restraint and moderation in the use of material goods, so we must not allow our desire to possess more material things to overtake our concern for the basic needs of people and the environment. Pope John Paul II has linked protecting the environment to "authentic human ecology," which can overcome "structures of sin" and which promotes both human dignity and respect for creation.[6] Technological innovation and entrepreneurship can help make possible options that can lead us to a more environmentally benign energy path. Changes in lifestyle based on traditional moral virtues can ease the way to a sustainable and equitable world economy in which sacrifice will no longer be an unpopular concept. For many of us, a life less focused on material gain may remind us that we are more than what we have. Rejecting the false promises of excessive or conspicuous consumption can even allow more time for family, friends, and civic responsibilities. A renewed sense of sacrifice and restraint could make an essential contribution to addressing global climate change.

PROTECTING THE ENVIRONMENT FOR FUTURE GENERATIONS

The common good calls us to extend our concern to future generations. Climate change poses the question "What does our generation owe to generations yet unborn?" As Pope John Paul II has written, "there is an order in the universe which must be respected, and . . . the human person, endowed with the capability of choosing freely, has a grave responsibility to preserve this order for the well-being of future generations."[7]

Passing along the problem of global climate change to future generations as a result of our delay, indecision, or self-interest would be easy. But we simply cannot leave this problem for the children of tomorrow. As stewards of their heritage, we have an obligation to respect their dignity and to pass on their natural inheritance, so that their lives are protected and, if possible, made better than our own.

POPULATION AND AUTHENTIC DEVELOPMENT

Population and climate change should be addressed from the broader perspective of a concern for protecting human life, caring for the environment, and respecting cultural norms and the religious faith and moral values of peoples. Population is not simply about statistics. Behind every demographic number is a precious and irreplaceable human life whose human dignity must be respected.

The global climate change debate cannot become just another opportunity for some groups—usually affluent advocates from the developed nations—to blame the problem on population growth in poor countries. Historically, the industrialized countries have emitted more greenhouse gases that warm the climate than have the developing countries. Affluent nations such as our own have to acknowledge the impact of voracious consumerism instead of simply calling for population and emissions controls from people in poorer nations.

A more responsible approach to population issues is the promotion of "authentic development," which represents a balanced view of human progress and includes respect for nature and social well-being.[8] Development policies that seek to reduce poverty with an emphasis on improved education and social conditions for women are far more effective than usual population reduction programs and far more respectful of women's dignity.[9]

We should promote a respect for nature that encourages policies fostering natural family planning and the education of women and men rather than coercive measures of population control or government incentives for birth control that violate local cultural and religious norms.

CARING FOR THE POOR AND ISSUES OF EQUITY

Working for the common good requires us to promote the flourishing of all human life and all of God's creation. In a special way, the common good requires solidarity with the poor who are often without the resources to face many problems, including the potential impacts of climate change. Our obligations to the one human family stretch across space and time. They tie us to the poor in our midst and across the globe, as well as to future generations. The commandment to love our neighbor invites us to consider the poor and marginalized of other nations as true brothers and sisters who share with us the one table of life intended by God for the enjoyment of all.

All nations share the responsibility to address the problem of global climate change. But historically the industrial economies have been responsible for the highest emissions of greenhouse gases that scientists suggest are causing the warming trend. Also, significant wealth, technological sophistication, and entrepreneurial creativity give these nations a greater capacity to find useful responses to this problem. To avoid greater impact, energy resource adjustments must be made both in the policies of richer countries and in the development paths of poorer ones.

Most people will agree that while the current use of fossil fuels has fostered and continues to foster substantial economic growth, development, and benefits for many, there is a legitimate concern that as developing countries improve their economies and emit more greenhouse gases, they will need technological help to mitigate further atmospheric environmental harm. Many of the poor in these countries live in degrading and desperate situations that often lead them to adopt environmentally harmful agricultural and industrial practices. In many cases, the heavy debt burdens, lack of trade opportunities, and economic inequities in the global market add to the environmental strains of the poorer countries. Developing countries have a right to economic development that can help lift people out of dire poverty. Wealthier industrialized nations have the resources, know-how, and entrepreneurship to produce more efficient cars and cleaner industries. These countries need to share these emerging technologies with the less-developed countries and assume more of the financial responsibility that would enable poorer countries to afford them. This would help developing countries adopt energy-efficient technologies more rapidly while still sustaining healthy economic growth and development.[10] Industries from the developed countries operating in developing nations should exercise a leadership role in preserving the environment.

No strategy to confront global climate change will succeed without the leadership and participation of the United States and other industrial nations. But any successful strategy must also reflect the genuine participation and concerns of those most affected and least able to bear the burdens. Developing and poorer nations must have a genuine place at the negotiating table. Genuine participation for those most affected is a moral and political necessity for advancing the common good.

The Public Policy Debate and Future Directions

C ATHOLIC SOCIAL TEACHING calls for bold and generous action on behalf of the common good. "Interdependence," as Pope John Paul II has written, "must be transformed into *solidarity*. . . . Surmounting every type of *imperialism* and determination to preserve their *own hegemony*, the stronger and richer nations must have a sense of moral *responsibility* for the other nations, so that a *real international system* may be established which will rest on the foundation of the *equality* of all peoples and on the necessary respect for their legitimate differences."[11]

The common good is built up or diminished by the quality of public debate. With its scientific, technological, economic, political, diplomatic, and religious dimensions, the challenge of global climate change may be a basic test of our democratic processes and political institutions. We respect the inquiry and dialogue that has been carried forward by a wide variety of scientists, diplomats, policy makers, and advocates, not only in the United States but around the world. These efforts should not be demeaned or distorted by disinformation or exaggeration. Serious dialogue should not be jeopardized by public relations tactics that fan fears or pit nations against one another. Leaders in every sector should seek to build a scientifically based consensus for the common good; avoid merely representing their own particular interests, industries, or movements; and act responsibly to protect future generations and the weak.

In the past decade, a continuing process of international diplomacy has led to agreements on principles and increasingly on procedures. In 1992, more than 160 nations, including the United States, ratified the first international treaty on global climate change at Earth Summit in Rio de Janeiro, Brazil, which was known as the United Nations Framework Convention on Climate Change (UNFCCC). In 1997, parties to the UNFCCC including the United States negotiated the Kyoto Protocol, which established mandatory emission reduction targets, market-based procedures for meeting those targets, and timetables for industrialized nations.

Without endorsing the specifics of these agreements and processes, we Catholic bishops acknowledge the development of these international negotiations and hope they and other future efforts can lead to just and effective progress. However, serious deliberations must continue to bring about prudent and effective actions to ensure equity among nations.

As an act of solidarity and in the interest of the common good, the United States should lead the developed nations in contributing to the sustainable economic development of poorer nations and to help build their capacity to ease climate change. Since our country's involvement is key to any resolution of these concerns, we call on our people and government to recognize the seriousness of the global warming threat and to develop effective policies that will diminish the possible consequences of global climate change. We encourage citizens to become informed participants in this important public debate. The measures we take today may not greatly moderate climate change in the near future, but they could make a significant difference for our descendants.

We also hope that the United States will continue to undertake reasonable and effective initiatives for energy conservation and the development of alternate renewable and clean-energy resources. New technologies and innovations can help meet this challenge. While more needs to be done to reduce air pollution, through the use of improved technologies and environmental entrepreneurship, the United States has made significant environmental gains over the last several decades. Our hope is that these technologies along with other resources can be shared with developing countries.

Within the United States, public policy should assist industrial sectors and workers especially impacted by climate change policies, and it should offer incentives to corporations to reduce greenhouse gas emissions and assistance to workers affected by these policies.

We encourage all parties to adopt an attitude of candor, conciliation, and prudence in response to serious, complex, and uncertain challenges. We hope the continuing dialogue within and among the diverse disciplines of science, economics, politics, and diplomacy will be guided by fundamental moral values: the universal common good, respect for God's creation, an option for the poor, and a sense of intergenerational obligation. Since religious values can enrich public discussion, this challenge offers opportunities for interfaith and ecumenical conversation and cooperation.

Finally, we wish to emphasize the need for personal conversion and responsibility. In our pastoral reflection *Renewing the Earth*, we wrote the following:

> Grateful for the gift of creation . . . we invite Catholics and men and women of good will in every walk of life to consider with us the moral issues raised by the environmental crisis. . . . These are matters of powerful urgency and major consequence. They constitute an exceptional call to conversion. As individuals, as institutions, as a people, we need a change of heart to preserve and protect the planet for our children and for generations yet unborn.[12]

Each of us should carefully consider our choices and lifestyles. We live in a culture that prizes the consumption of material goods. While the poor often have too little, many of us can be easily caught up in a frenzy of wanting more and more—a bigger home, a larger car, etc. Even though energy resources literally fuel our economy and provide a good quality of life, we need to ask about ways we can conserve energy, prevent pollution, and live more simply.

Conclusion

OUR NATIONAL DEBATE over solutions to global climate change needs to move beyond the uses and abuses of science, sixty-second ads, and exaggerated claims. Because this issue touches so many people, as well as the planet itself, all parties need to strive for a civil and constructive debate about US decisions and leadership in this area.

As people of religious faith, we bishops believe that the atmosphere that supports life on earth is a God-given gift, one we must respect and protect. It unites us as one human family. If we harm the atmosphere, we dishonor our Creator and the gift of creation. The values of our faith call us to humility, sacrifice, and a respect for life and the natural gifts God has provided. Pope John Paul II reminds us in his statement *The Ecological Crisis: A Common Responsibility* that "respect for life and for the dignity of the human person extends also to the rest of creation, which is called to join man in praising God."[13] In that spirit of praise and thanksgiving to God for the wonders of creation, we Catholic bishops call for a civil dialogue and prudent and constructive action to protect God's precious gift of the earth's atmosphere with a sense of genuine solidarity and justice for all God's children.

Notes

1. John Paul II, *On the Hundredth Anniversary of Rerum Novarum (Centesimus Annus)* (Washington, DC: United States Catholic Conference, 1991), no. 38.

2. John Paul II, "International Solidarity Needed to Safeguard Environment," address by the Holy Father to the European Bureau for the Environment, *L'Osservatore Romano* (June 26, 1996).

3. John Paul II, *The Ecological Crisis: A Common Responsibility* (Washington, DC: United States Catholic Conference, 1990), no. 6.

4. John Paul II, *On the Hundredth Anniversary of Rerum Novarum*, no. 32.

5. John Paul II, *On Social Concern (Sollicitudo Rei Socialis)* (Washington, DC: United States Catholic Conference, 1988), no. 42.

6. John Paul II, *On the Hundredth Anniversary of Rerum Novarum*, no. 38.

7. John Paul II, "The Exploitation of the Environment Threatens the Entire Human Race," address to the Vatican symposium on the environment (1990), in *Ecology and Faith: The Writings of Pope John Paul II*, ed. Sr. Ancilla Dent, OSB (Berkhamsted, England: Arthur James, 1997), 12.

8. John Paul II, *On Social Concern*, ch. four. This chapter of the encyclical gives a more complete definition of the concept of authentic development.

9. Second Vatican Council, *Pastoral Constitution on the Church in the Modern World (Gaudium et Spes)*, nos. 50-51, in Austin Flannery, ed., *Vatican Council II: The Conciliar and Post Conciliar Documents*, new rev. ed., 1st vol. (Northport, NY: Costello Publishing, 1996).

10. See also treatment of this topic in *Stewardship: A Disciple's Response* (Washington, DC: United States Catholic Conference, 1993), 27.

11. Ibid., no. 39.

12. United States Catholic Conference, *Renewing the Earth: An Invitation to Reflection and Action on Environment in Light of Catholic Social Teaching* (Washington, DC: United States Catholic Conference, 1992), 3. See also treatment of this theme in *Stewardship: A Disciple's Response*, 46.

13. John Paul II, *The Ecological Crisis*, no. 16.

The Science of
Global Climate Change

The photographs from the Apollo missions show earth glowing in the still-ness of space like a blue-white opal on black velvet. Cool and beautiful, it hurries along in the sun's gravitational embrace. The earth is our home, our whole wide world.

Our enfolding blanket of air, our atmosphere, is both the physical condi-tion for human community and its most compelling symbol. We all breathe the same air. Guarding the integrity of the atmosphere—without which complex life could not have evolved on this planet—seems like common sense. Yet a broad consensus of modern science is that human activ-ity is beginning to alter the earth's atmospheric characteristics in serious, perhaps profound ways. For the past century, researchers have been gathering and verifying data that reveal an increase in the global average temperature. Until recently, scientists could not say with great confidence whether or not this phenomenon was in any way the result of human activity or entirely the result of natural changes over time.

To deal with the difficulty of making precise measurements and arriving at definite conclusions, the World Meteorological Organization and the United Nations Environment Programme established the Intergovernmental Panel on Climate Change (IPCC) to seek a clear explanation of the causes and possible impacts of this global climate change.[1] Because of the large number of scientists involved in the IPCC and its process of consultation, its reports are considered widely as offering the most authoritative scientific perspectives on the issue. IPCC's findings have met with general—but because of remaining uncertainties, not complete—agreement within the wider scientific community.

In 1996, the IPCC issued its Second Assessment Reports, which summarized the current state of knowledge. The first of these reports concluded that *"the bal-ance of evidence suggests that there is a discernible human influence on global climate."* [2] The Third Assessment Reports, approved in early 2001, found even stronger evidence and concluded, *"most of the observed warming over the last 50 years is likely to have been due to the [human-induced] increase in greenhouse gas concentrations"* (italics added). [3]

The IPCC offers convincing evidence that there exists if not a clear and present danger then a clear and future one, and that coming changes will affect all aspects of the environment and societal well-being. Based on measurements taken over both land and sea, the global average surface-air temperature has increased by about one degree Fahrenheit since 1860, building up as the Industrial Revolution was hitting full stride. While this is hardly a frightening increase for a particular geographic location, the temperature change is global in extent, so one must read it against the background of the earth's average temperature during historic times. According to IPCC, the rate and duration of warming in the twentieth century appears to be the largest in the last one thousand years. The twentieth century also experienced precipitation increases in mid- and high-northern latitudes; drier conditions in the subtropics; decreases in snow cover, mountain glaciers, and Arctic sea ice; and a rise of four to eight inches in mean sea level. [4]

The "greenhouse effect," though complex in detail, is simple enough in outline. Not considering the internal heating due to radioactive decay and volcanism, the earth draws its thermal energy from the sun. Atmospheric gases form a protective cover that makes our planet hospitable to life, transmitting visible light, blocking out harmful high-energy radiation like ultraviolet rays, and keeping temperatures comfortable by moderating the escape of heat into space. However, the precise mix of these gases is quite delicate, and changing that mix alters the atmosphere's properties. An increase in the relative abundance of the greenhouse gases (carbon dioxide, methane, chlorofluorocarbons, tropospheric ozone, and nitrous oxide) causes the earth to trap more of the sun's heat, resulting in what is called "global warming." Since the beginning of the industrial period, the IPCC reports, the concentration of the principal greenhouse gas, carbon dioxide, has increased by 30 percent and is now greater than at any time in the past 20 million years. [5] The presence of methane (150 percent increase) and nitrous oxide (16 percent increase) is also growing. The result is the small but alarming temperature rise science has detected.[6]

What causes greenhouse gases to accumulate in the atmosphere? Emissions from cars and trucks, industry and electric plants, and businesses and homes are the largest part of the answer, although other factors such as deforestation contribute. The Industrial Revolution was built on furnaces and engines burning fossil fuels (coal, natural gas, oil, and such derived products as gasoline and heating oil). These fossil fuels now power the U.S. and global economy. Although some of the smoke particles and other pollutants (such as sulfur dioxide) now streaming from chimneys and tailpipes can actually cool the earth if they take an aerosol form, the great bulk of our emissions are contributing a warming influence. Reflecting upon studies completed since its last report in 1996, the IPCC says, "There is new and stronger evidence that most of the warming observed over the last 50 years is attributable to human activities."[7]

Whatever the extent, severity, or geographical distribution of global warming impacts, the problem is expected to disproportionately affect the poor, the vulnerable, and generations yet unborn. Projected sea level rises could impact low-lying coastal areas in densely populated nations of the developing world. Storms are most likely to strain the fragile housing infrastructure of the poorest nations. The migration of diseases could further challenge the presently inadequate health care systems of these same nations. Droughts or floods, it is feared, will afflict regions already too often hit by famine, hunger, and malnutrition. Because the number of days with high heat and humidity are likely to increase, heat stress impacts will also increase, especially among the elderly, the sick, children, and the poor.[8]

The scientific reports of the IPCC portray the long-term challenge global climate change poses. Its findings, while not complete, are widely accepted in the scientific community. In June 2001, the National Academy of Sciences released a report, prepared at the request of President Bush, summarizing a prestigious panel's understanding of global climate change and an assessment of the work of the International Panel on Climate Change. The panel said that "greenhouse gases are accumulating in the Earth's atmosphere as a result of human activities." It also found that "we cannot rule out that some significant part of these changes are also a reflection of natural variability. . . . Because there is considerable uncertainty in current understanding of how the climate system varies naturally and reacts to emissions of greenhouse gases and aerosols, current estimates of the magnitude of future warming should be regarded as tentative and subject to future adjustments (either upward or downward)." The report noted that while the full implications of climate change remain unknown, the panel "generally agrees with the assessment of human-caused change presented in the IPCC Working Group I scientific report."[9]

---

1. To date, the IPCC's work represents the most authoritative estimates and prognosis of current and future climate change data. This statement utilizes the following Second and Third Assessment Reports by the IPCC:

 1996a: *Climate Change 1995: The Science of Climate Change. Contribution of Working Group I to the Second Assessment Report of the Intergovernmental Panel on Climate Change*, eds. J. T. Houghton, L. G. Meira Filho, B. A. Callander, N. Harris, A. Kattenberg, and K. Maskell (Cambridge and New York: Cambridge University Press).

 1996b: *Climate Change 1995: Impacts, Adaptations and Mitigation of Climate Change: Scientific-Technical Analyses. Contribution of Working Group II to the Second Assessment Report of the Intergovernmental Panel on Climate Change*, eds. R. T. Watson, M. C. Zinyowera, and R. H. Moss (Cambridge and New York: Cambridge University Press).

 1996c: *Climate Change 1995: Economic and Social Dimensions of Climate Change. Contribution of Working Group III to the Second Assessment Report of the Intergovernmental Panel on Climate Change*, eds. J. P. Bruce, Hoesund Kee, and E. F. Haites (Cambridge and New York: Cambridge University Press).

 1996d: *The IPCC Second Assessment Synthesis of Scientific-Technical Information Relevant to Interpreting Article 2 of the UN Framework Convention on Climate Change* (Geneva: World Meteorological Organization/United Nations Environment Programme).

 2001a: *Climate Change 2001: The Scientific Basis*, eds. J. T. Houghton, Y. Ding, D. J. Griggs, M. Noguer, P. van der Linden, X. Dai, K. Maskell, and C. Johnson (Cambridge and New York: Cambridge University Press).

 2001b: *Climate Change 2001: Impacts, Adaptation, and Vulnerability*, eds. J. McCarthy, O. Canziani, N. Leary, D. Dokken, and K. White (Cambridge and New York: Cambridge University Press).

 2001c: *Climate Change 2001: Mitigation*, eds. O. Davidson, B. Metz, R. Swart, and J. Pan (Cambridge and New York: Cambridge University Press).

2.   IPCC, 1996a, 5.

3.   IPCC, 2001a, 10.

4.   Ibid., ch. two.

5.   Ibid., 7.

6.   Ibid.

7.   Ibid., 10.

8.   IPCC, 2001b.

9.   National Academy of Science, *Climate Change Science: An Analysis of Some Key Questions* (Washington, D.C., June 7, 2001).